To Nannow with
all my love.
You are the best
Grandmother ever.

Max

Grandmothers

are
Forever

Dr. Criswell Freeman

Simon & Schuster, Inc.
New York London Toronto Sydney

Simon & Schuster, Inc.
1230 Avenue of the Americas, New York, New York 10020

© 2006 Freeman-Smith, LLC.
The quoted ideas expressed in this book (but not Scripture verses) are not, in all cases, exact quotations, as some have been edited for clarity and brevity. In all cases, the author has attempted to maintain the speaker's original intent. In some cases, quoted material for this book was obtained from secondary sources, primarily print media. While every effort was made to ensure the accuracy of these sources, the accuracy cannot be guaranteed. For additions, deletions, corrections, or clarifications in future editions of this text, please write Freeman-Smith, LLC.

All scripture quotations are taken from:

NIV® are from the *Holy Bible, New International Version*®. Copyright © 1973, 1978, 1984 by International Bible Society. Used by permission of Zondervan Publishing House. All rights reserved.

Cover Design & Page Layout by Bart Dawson

Manufactured in the United States of America

10 9 8 7 6 5 4 3 2 1

ISBN-13: 978-1-4169-2573-6
ISBN-10: 1-4169-2573-2

For Virginia Criswell, Marie Freeman,
and Angie Knight

Table of Contents

Introduction

This book pays tribute to grandmothers everywhere. And with good cause. Grandmothers reshape eternity through their influence on future generations. But, this is as it should be because without grandmothers, there would be no future generations to influence.

In my own case, I am continually blessed by the lives of two special women, my own grandmothers: Virginia Criswell and Marie Freeman. My grandmothers helped shape me in ways that I am only now beginning to understand. And, the more I learn about myself, the more I understand the priceless gift of caring, loving grandparents.

So if you happen to be a grandmother, thank you for all you have done and continue to do. And if you happen to be a grandchild sneaking a peak at Grandma's quotation book, remember that grandmothers are forever. And, remember that all you are you owe to your grandmother...in more ways than one.

Chapter 1
Grandmothers Are...

Grandmother is just another name for love.

—

Old-Time Saying

$\mathcal{T}$he dictionary defines the word "grandmother" as "the mother of one's father or mother." But thoughtful grandchildren know that the true meaning of the word "grandmother" can never be defined so easily.

A grandmother is usually asked to assume many roles: She is teacher, confidante, babysitter, family historian, spiritual advisor, family counselor and short-order cook. A grandmother is the foundation of the family, often the glue that holds the clan together. She guides her children and grandchildren by serving as role model and advice-giver of last resort.

On the pages that follow, we pay tribute to the women who keep grateful grandchildren thanking their lucky stars for their great grandmothers.

A grandparent is like a wise elder,
more detached than a parent.
—Richard Walker

Grandparents are our living link to the past.
—George Bush, Sr.

If a family has no grandparent,
it possesses no jewel.
—Chinese Proverb

Being a grandmother is above all
a learning experience.
—Sheila Kitzinger

Grandmothers are the bearers of tradition.

—Judith Stevens-Long

A grandparent is a unique kind of
emotionally involved,
part-time parent without pressure.

—Dr. Fitzhugh Dodson

I thank God for my grandmother who stood
on the word of God and lived with the spirit
of courage and grace.

—Maya Angelou

Her children arise up, and call her blessed.

—Proverbs 31:28

We learn to be grandmothers, just as
we learn to be mothers.

—Sheila Kitzinger

Grandparents are the family watchdogs.

—Lillian E. Troll

If you would civilize a man, begin with
his grandmother.

—Victor Hugo

Grandparents have a special kind of love.

—Eda LeShan

Almost all grandmothers agree that
grandparenting is easier than parenting.

—Judith Stevens-Long

Becoming a grandmother brings
the satisfaction of giving and receiving love,
sometimes more freely
and more generously than ever before.

—Shelia Kitzinger

The connection between grandparents and
grandchild is natural and second
in emotional power only to the bond
between parent and child.

—Arthur Kornhaber

A grandmother is a person who has time.
>—Anonymous child's definition

Grandparents are more patient,
more tolerant, more aware of little changes
in their grandchild.
>—Nancy Reagan

Grandma was a first-aid station who
restored us to health by her amazing faith.
>—Lillian Smith

Grandmothers Last A Lifetime...And Beyond

Lin Yutang observed, "Of all the rights of women, the greatest is to be a mother." And, if motherhood is the world's greatest privilege, surely grand-motherhood is among the world's greatest delights.

The role of grandmother can be a joyful experience indeed, but wise grandmothers do much more than simply play with their grandchildren or baby-sit them. Thoughtful grandmothers serve as enduring, lifelong role models.

Through words and deeds, a grandmother's influence extends beyond time and space, weaving itself as an unbroken thread through future generations. In truth, a grandmother's impact upon her family lasts a lifetime...and beyond.

Happiness is being a grandmother.

—

Jan Stoop and Betty Southard

Chapter 2
Grandchildren Are...

Perfect love does not sometimes come until the first grandchild.

—

Welsh Proverb

Grandchildren are bountiful blessings to the grandparents who, without direct parental control, can usually enjoy their offspring at a safe distance. Herein, we explore the joys of observing, teaching and loving the children's children. May they live happily ever after.

When a grandchild is born, all relationships
in the family shift and change.

—Sheila Kitzinger

When you have a grandchild,
you have two children.

—Yiddish Saying

Give a little love to a child and you get
a great deal back.

—John Ruskin

Every child who comes into the world
presents a new possibility for lifting
the destiny of the human race.

—Anna B. Mow

Every child's relationship with a close and
loving grandparent is unique.

—Arthur Kornhaber

There was never a child so lovely but
his mother was glad to get him asleep.

—Ralph Waldo Emerson

Blessed be childhood, which brings down
something of heaven into the midst
of our rough earthliness.

—Henri Frédéric Amiel

Wherever children are,
there is the golden age.

—Novalis

A sweet child is the sweetest thing
in nature.

—Charles Lamb

In the eyes of its grandmother,
every beetle is a gazelle.

—African Proverb

Your sons weren't made to like you.
That's what grandchildren are for.

—Jane Smiley

Grandchildren Are . . .

A grandchild is a bundle of love wrapped in possibilities. No wonder that every grandbaby is the light of grandma's eyes.

Henry Ward Beecher proclaimed, "Children are the hands by which we take hold of heaven." A grandmother, by taking firm hold of her grandchild's hand, creates a little piece of heaven here on earth.

*The secret of life is to skip
having children and go
directly to grandchildren.*
—

Mell Lazarus

Chapter 3
Love

*A grandmother's love
is like no other love
in the world.*

—

Old-Time Saying

A grandmother's love is a wonderful thing for grandmoms and grandkids alike. A grandchild who has been lucky enough to feel the secure love of a caring grandparent will never forget that experience. And, a grandparent who feels the touch of an adoring grandchild is changed forever.

Love is the currency by which life is denominated, a currency that is multiplied as it is spent. And, as we all know, when it comes to this currency of love, grandmothers are biggest of the big-time spenders. Thank goodness!

Love doesn't make the world go round.
Love is what makes the ride worthwhile.
—Franklin P. Jones

There is a net of love by which
you can catch souls.
—Mother Teresa

Love is the river of life in the world.
—Henry Ward Beecher

There is only one terminal dignity—love.
—Helen Hayes

The closest friends I have made all through
life have been people who also grew up
close to a loved and loving grandfather
and grandmother.

—Margaret Mead

Love doesn't sit there like a stone,
it has to be made like bread;
remade all the time; made new.

—Ursula K. LeGuin

Love stretches your heart and
makes you big inside.

—Margaret Walker

Confidence is the best proof of love.
—Maria Edgeworth

There is nothing so loyal as love.
—Alice Cary

If one wishes to know love,
one must live love.
—Leo Buscaglia

To love is to receive a glimpse of heaven.
—Karen Sunde

You can give without loving,
　　but you cannot love without giving.
　　　　　　　　　　—Amy Charmichael

Love does not dominate; it cultivates.
　　　　　　　　　　—Goethe

Love is shown by deeds, not words.
　　　　　　　　　　—Philippine Proverb

To love abundantly is to live abundantly,
and to love forever is to live forever.

—Anonymous

When we come right down to it,
the secret to having it all is loving it all.

—Dr. Joyce Brothers

To love children is to love God.

—Roy Rogers

A Grandmother's Love

Grandmothers understand the power of love, and they share that message with the entire family. A grandmother shares her love through words and—more importantly—through deeds. The beneficiaries of that love are forever blessed.

A grandmother's love becomes her permanent legacy, her timeless gift to the family. It is a gift to her children, to her grandchildren, and to subsequent generations.

You will find, as you look back upon your life, that the moments when you have really lived are the moments when you have done things in the spirit of love.

—

Henry Drummond

Chapter 4
Home

Home is the place where the great are small and the small are great.

—

Robert Savage

*I*t has been said that "home is where the heart is." It must be added that a grandchild's second home is where grandmother is. Fortunate kids build lifelong memories around the fun and games at Grandmother's.

In this chapter, we examine some of the essential elements of a happy, functional home. And, we learn what savvy grandmoms have known all the while: A real home is any building built upon a foundation of love.

It takes a heap o' lovin' in a house
        to make it a home.

                    —Edgar A. Guest

A house is not a home.

                      —Polly Adler

A house is no home unless it contains food
and fire for the mind as well as for the body.

                   —Margaret Fuller

Home—that blessed word which opens
        to the human heart the most
        perfect glimpse of Heaven.

                 —Lydia M. Child

Houses are like the hearts of men, I think,
They must have life within. They must have
fires and friends and kin, love for the day
and night, children in strong, young laps.
Then they have life.

—Lenora Speyer

Everyone has, I think, in some quiet corner
of his mind, an ideal home waiting to
become a reality.

—Paige Rense

I have been very happy with my homes,
but homes are no more than the people
who live in them.

—Nancy Reagan

Home is not a way station:
It is the profession of faith in life.
—Sol Chaneles

It takes a hundred men to make
an encampment but one woman
to make a home.
—Robert Ingersoll

The woman who creates and sustains
a home is a creator second only to God.
—Helen Hunt Jackson

Make two homes for thyself: one actual
home and another spiritual home which
thou art to carry with thee always.
—St. Catherine of Siena

Home ought to be our clearinghouse,
the place from which we go forth lessoned
and disciplined, and ready for life.
—Kathleen Norris

Home is where you learn values.
It's the responsibility of the family.
—Melba Moore

*Home is where
the heart is.*
—

Pliny the Elder

Home Is...

Home is not simply a place; it is a state of mind, built as much with love as with brick and mortar. The size of a house is relatively unimportant; the collective size of the hearts that dwell inside is all-important.

What is a home? It is a place where we are protected and loved. It is a place where we are free to be ourselves. It is a place where we celebrate our victories and find comfort in our defeats. Home is the place where we gather together with loved ones and share this wonderful gift called life. In other words, home is just about the very best place on earth.

Home wasn't built

in a day.

—

Jane Ace

Chapter 5
Family

*The strength of a nation derives
from the integrity of the home.*
—
Confucius

Grandmothers, having raised the children who raise the children, possess special insights into family life. So when it comes to matters of house and home, wise kids and grandkids seek the advice of their clan's most experienced mother.

The observations, tips, and common-sense advice in this chapter are intended for families everywhere. And, if these words sound suspiciously like those uttered by grandmother, so be it. After all, grandmother knows best.

When the whole family is together,
the soul is in place.

—Russian Proverb

If I were starting my family over again,
I would give first priority to my wife
and children, not to my work.

—Richard Halverson

Marriage is a covered dish.

—Swiss Proverb

A happy family is but an earlier heaven.

—Sir John Bowring

A successful marriage requires falling in love
many times, always with the same person.
—Mignon McLaughlin

Marriage is not just spiritual communion
and passionate embraces; marriage is also
three meals a day, sharing the workload,
and remembering to carry out the trash.
—Dr. Joyce Brothers

No kingdom divided can stand—
neither can a household.
—Christine de Pisan

A successful marriage is not a gift;
it is an achievement.
—Ann Landers

When a marriage works, nothing on earth
can take its place.

—Helen Gahagan Douglas

Better a hundred enemies outside the house
than one inside.

—Arabian Proverb

What we learn within the family are
the most unforgettable lessons that
our lives will ever teach us.

—Maggie Scarf

Loving Our Families

When Mother Teresa received her Nobel Prize, she was asked, "What can we do to promote world peace?" She replied, "Go home and love your family." That's powerful advice for parents and grandparents alike.

No duty is more important than that of loving and caring for our families. When we give of our time, our energy, and our love, the next generation reaps rich rewards...and so do we.

*A bonus of being
a grandmother is being with
babies and toddlers —
and rediscovering the delights
of play.*

—

Shelia Kitzinger

Chapter 6
The Younger
Generation

Every generation revolts against its parents and makes friends with its grandparents.

—

Lewis Mumford

*E*very generation is the same, only different. But sometimes, parents are simply too close to the firing line to realize that their kids are not so unlike themselves. Mom and dad may panic, fearing that their children are irresponsible, strange, or worse. What's needed is perspective. And who better to provide this perspective than grandmother? After all, she's a card-carrying member of the generation that has "seen it all" and lived to tell about it.

Grandparents understand that the more kids change, the more they remain the same. So parents take notice: Your children have the same hopes and dreams that you had at their age. But as for the hairstyles and clothing, well that's an entirely different matter.

Youth is wholly experimental.
—Robert Louis Stevenson

Youth, even in its sorrows, always has
a brillancy of its own.
—Victor Hugo

Beautiful is youth because it
never comes again.
—George Jean Nathan

When you're young, the silliest notions
seem the greatest achievements.
—Pearl Bailey

Youth is the time of life when one believes
he is immortal.
—William Hazlitt

Young folks will have their own way.
—Martha Washington

Children are all foreigners.
—Ralph Waldo Emerson

Children are like clocks...
they must be allowed to run.
—James Dobson

Don't panic even during the storms
of adolescence. Better times are ahead.

—James Dobson

Don't limit a child to your own learning
for he was born in another time.

—Rabbinic Saying

Children need love, especially when they
do not deserve it.

—Harold S. Hulbert

We cannot always build the future for
our youth, but we can build our youth
for the future.

—Franklin D. Roosevelt

Children have more need of models
than of critics.

—Joseph Joubert

What children learn at home is what
they will take with them when
they are grown.

—Chuck Christensen

Parents, grandparents, and children each
have something to give each other.

—Fitzhugh Dodson

When you listen to your children,
you are paying them a compliment.
By listening, you increase their feelings of
self-respect and self-worth.

—Dean and Grace Merrill

It's hard to know where one generation ends and the other begins. But it's somewhere around nine o'clock at night.

—

Charles Ruffing

Chapter 7

Life

Life is what we make it.

Always has been;

always will be.

—

Grandma Moses

*L*ife is a great mystery to us all, grandmothers excluded. Somehow, somewhere, grandmothers just figured things out. Thankfully, they are always willing to share their hard-earned knowledge—if the younger generation is willing to slow down long enough to listen.

This chapter contains grandmotherly advice about life. Kids, grandkids, great-grandkids, even casual bystanders, please take notice!

Write it on your heart that every day is
the best day of the year.
—Ralph Waldo Emerson

Don't anticipate the happiness
of tomorrow. Discover it today.
—Ella Wheeler Wilcox

I could never be content to simply look on.
Life was meant to be lived. We must never,
for any reason, turn our backs on life.
—Eleanor Roosevelt

Life is a party; you join after it's started and
you leave before it's finished.
—Elsa Maxwell

Life is right now.

—Barbara Bush

To live is to fight, to suffer and to love.

—Elizabeth Leseur

It is important to stay close enough to
the pulse of life to feel its rhythm,
to be comforted by its steadiness,
to know that life is vital, and one's own
minute living a torn fragment
of the larger cloth.

—Marjorie Kinnan Rawlings

God has a plan for all of us, but
He expects us to do our share of the work.

—Minnie Pearl

The life that doesn't have a sense
of responsibility to something broader
than one's self is not much of a life.

—Gail Sheehy

Life begets life. Energy creates energy.
It is by spending oneself that
one becomes rich.

—Sarah Bernhardt

We can learn so much from vital older
women who live their passions
with purpose and direction.

—Gail Sheehy

Love the moment and the energy of the
moment will be spread beyond
all boundaries.

—Corita Kent

The spiritual eyesight improves
as the physical eyesight declines.

—Plato

All the flowers of all the tomorrows are
in the seeds of today.

—Anne Outland

What we are is God's gift to us.
What we become is our gift to God.

—Eleanor Powell

Most things have an escape clause,
      but children are forever.

                    —Lewis Grizzard

Children are the messages we will send to
      a time we will never see.

                    —Neil Postman

It's never too late—in fiction or in life—
      to revise.

                    —Nancy Thayer

We are here to help one another
      along life's journey.

                    —William Bennett

The Gift of Life

Having given the gift of life, who better to explain it than grandmothers? And, make no mistake about it: life is indeed a gift—courtesy of our mothers and grandmothers—a gift that should be treasured and used to the fullest.

Grandmothers view life with the wisdom that is gained through years of experience. They realize that life can be—and should be—a work of art. And, savvy grandmoms help their kids make each day—and each life—a masterpiece.

Each day comes bearing its own gifts. Untie the ribbons.

—

Ruth Ann Schabacker

Chapter 8
Memories

God gave us memories that we might have roses in December.

—

James M. Barrie

*I*t has been said that memory is the thing we forget with. But, some memories are simply too priceless to lose. Happy remembrances of days gone by compose the fabric of life; they make us who we are. Other memories, those that breed bitterness or regret, are best discarded with vigor and haste.

The lessons in this chapter teach us that a retentive memory can be a blessing or a curse, depending upon how it is used. So all of us are advised to do what savvy grandmothers do: we should practice the art of memory management, because we can never be fully contented until we remember to forget the things that don't need remembering. And vice versa.

No man can know where he is going
unless he knows exactly where he's been.

—Maya Angelou

Look at the past. Don't hide from it.
It will not catch you if you don't repeat it.

—Pearl Bailey

Lord, keep my memory green.

—Charles Dickens

Remember childhood visions.

—Mary McCleod Bethune

Memory moderates prosperity, decreases
adversity, controls youth and
delights old age.

—Lactantius

To be able to enjoy one's past is to
live twice.

—Martial

Relationships with other people have
made my life incredibly rich.

—Barbara Bush

The little present must not be allowed
wholly to elbow the great past
out of our view.

—Andrew Lang

Women and elephants never forget.
—Dorothy Parker

A retentive memory may be a good thing,
but the ability to forget is the true token
of greatness.
—Elbert Hubbard

Make it a rule of life never to regret and
never to look back. Regret is an appalling
waste of energy; you can't build on it;
it is only good for wallowing in.
—Katherine Mansfield

The things we remember best are those
better forgotten.
—Baltasar Gracián

How we remember, what we remember,
and why we remember form the most
personal map of our individuality.
—Christina Baldwin

Memory is the diary we all carry within us.
—Mary H. Waldrip

Friends fill the memory with sweet things.
—Martha Washington

In memory each of us is an artist;
each of us creates.
—Patricia Hampt

Some folks never exaggerate—
they just remember big.
—Audrey Snead

*Grandmothers
are full of memories.*
—

Margaret Walker

Lessons in Faith

Grandmothers, having seen it all more than once, understand the power of faith. As Grandmoms know all too well, faith is the foundation upon which great lives are built. Faith is a gift we give ourselves that pays rich dividends in good times or bad.

Wise grandmothers teach the power of faith by word and by example. When they do, fortunate grandchildren learn that faith protects...and perfect faith protects perfectly.

*Grandparents are
the living link
to the family's past.*
—

Arthur Kornhaber

Chapter 9
Raising Grandkids

The secret of dealing successfully with a child is not to be its parent.

—

Mell Lazarus

$\mathcal{M}$ost grandparents help raise their grandchildren at arm's length. In such cases, a little distance can be a very healthy thing. Because parents' parents are usually somewhat removed from the daily grind of child-rearing, they can offer counsel with a certain degree of objectivity. Such level-headed advice is badly needed since parental objectivity, as we all know, is a commodity much rarer than gold.

In this chapter, we examine ways that grandparents make a difference in the lives of their grandkids...a big difference.

If grandparents want to have a meaningful
and constructive role, they must learn that
becoming a grandparent is not having
a second chance at parenthood.

—Eda LeShan

Never tell your children how to
raise their children.

—Fitzhugh Dodson

An important goal for grandparents
is not to compete with parents.

—Eda LeShan

Very rarely will you make a mistake by
keeping quiet about something concerning
your grandchildren.

—Fitzhugh Dodson

A child's education should begin at least
a hundred years before he is born.
—Oliver Wendell Holmes, Sr.

A great gift to one's child is knowledge.
—Christine de Pisan

Education is the jewel casting brilliance
into the future.
—Mari Evans

The potential possibilities of any child are
the most intriguing and stimulating
in all creation.
—Ray L Wilbur

Inspire youngsters to develop the talent
they possess.

—Augusta Savage

Those who are lifting the world upward
and onward are those who encourage
more than criticize.

—Elisabeth Harrison

Teaching is the art of assisting discovery.

—Mark Van Doren

Children have to educated, but they also
have to be left to educate themselves.

—Abbé Dimnet

Learning in childhood is like engraving
on a rock.

—Arabian Proverb

As the twig is bent, so the tree grows.

—Virgil

Trees bend only when young.

—Jewish Saying

What children learn at home is what they
will take with them when they are grown.

—Chuck Christensen

His heritage to his children wasn't words or
possessions, but an unspoken treasure,
the treasure of his example as
a man and a father.

—Will Rogers, Jr.

Children have never been very good at
listening to their elders, but they have
never failed to imitate them.

—James Baldwin

Children are very much aware of integrity;
when they see it they know it, though they
wouldn't know the word.

—Eudora Welty

He who lives well is the best teacher.

—Cervantes

Education is life, not books.

—African Proverb

Our children observe us all day long,
at our best and at our worst. Much of what
they learn comes simply from living
with us and observing us.

—Shirley Suderman

To teach good behavior one wisely
understands that young people must
play and laugh.

—Christine de Pisan

The most deprived children are those
who have to do nothing in order to get
what they want.

—Sydney J. Harris

Do not handicap your children
by making their lives easy.

—Lazarus Long

At every step the child should be allowed
to meet the real experiences of life;
the thorns should never be plucked
from his roses.

—Ellen Key

Never help a child with a task at which
he feels he can succeed.

—Maria Montessori

You must teach your children to dream
with their eyes open.
—Harry Edwards

The goal of disciplining our children is to
encourage their growth as respectful,
responsible, self-disciplined individuals.
—Don H. Highlander

Loving a child doesn't mean giving in to all
his whims; to love him is to bring
out the best in him, to teach him to
love what is difficult.
—Nadia Boulanger

Remember, when they have a tantrum,
don't have one of your own.
—Judith Kurisansky

Good grandparenting begins early,
long before the birth of the first grandchild.
—Arthur Kornhaber

When women talk about their own
grandmothers, the thing they value most was
the grandmother's willingness to listen.
—Sheila Kitzinger

When you are dealing with a child,
keep your wits about you and sit on the floor.
—Austin O'Malley

Don't take up someone's time talking about
the smartness of your grandchildren. He
wants to talk about the smartness of his.
—E. W. Howe

Take responsibility for the future of society
by raising responsible children.

—Kaye Gibson

Never argue with a child or a fool.

—American Saying

Wherever children are learning,
there dwells the Divine Presence.

—Old Saying

Was there ever a grandparent tired after
a day of minding noisy youngsters, who
hasn't felt the Lord knew what he was doing
when he gave little children to young people?

—Joe E. Wells

*L*ittle children have big ears.

—

American Saying

Chapter 10
Forever Young

As soon as you feel too old to do a thing, do it.

—

Margaret Deland

*Y*outh is transitory, but a youthful spirit need never grow old. On the pages that follow, we consider a checklist of proven ways to retain or regain that youthful spirit.

The ideas in this chapter compose the roadmap to a bubbling fountain of youth that exists within all of us. It is a fountain of our own construction; how we drink depends upon how we think.

Youth has no age.

—Pablo Picasso

Life before 50 is nothing but a warm-up.

—Advertisement for AARP

Though it sounds absurd, it is true to say
I felt younger at sixty than I felt at twenty.

—Ellen Glasgow

My interest is in the future because
I'm going to spend the rest of my life there.

—Charles F. Kettering

Grandparenting is a marvelous opportunity
to keep alive, alert, growing and giving.

—Fitzhugh Dodson

The secret to longevity is keeping active
all the time.

—Milton Berle

Keeping busy is the answer.

—Marjory Stoneman Douglas
On her 100th birthday

Painting is not important.
The important thing is keeping busy.

—Grandma Moses

Nobody ought to be too old to improve.
—Anna Letitia Barbauld

You don't grow old; when you cease to grow,
you are old.
—Charles Judson Herrick

If we don't change, we don't grow.
If we don't grow, we are not really living.
—Gail Sheehy

Only in growth, reform and change,
paradoxically enough, is true security found.
—Anne Morrow Lindbergh

Change is the constant, the signal for
rebirth, the egg of the phoenix.
—Christina Baldwin

There are very few things you can do to defy
the aging process. Keeping your hopes alive
is definitely one of them.
—Stanley H. Cath

Of all the things you wear, your expression
is the most important.
—Janet Lane

Wrinkles should merely indicate
where smiles have been.
—Mark Twain

Aging slowly does not mean doing battle
with the passing years.
It means enjoying them to the hilt.

—Myron Brenton

Activity does not wear out the human
machine and spirit...inactivity does.

—Garson Kanin

The excitement of learning separates you
from old age. As long as you're learning,
you're not old.

—Rosalyn S. Yalow

Age is bothersome only when you stop
to coddle it.

—Maurice Chevalier

Anyone who keeps the ability to see beauty
never grows old.

—Franz Kafka

All that is good in man lies in youthful
feeling and mature thought.

—Joseph Joubert

You are only young once, and if you work
it right, once is enough.

—Joe E. Lewis

There's the beauty of age, more profound,
more complete. It forms a fine patina that
only life and living can impart.

—Karen Westerberg Reyes

The first forty years of life give us the text:
the next thirty supply the commentary.

—Schopenhauer

In youth we learn. In age we understand.

—Marie Ebner-Eschenbach

The evening of life brings with it its lamp.

—Joseph Joubert

All that I know I learned after I was thirty.

—Georges Clemenceau

Middle age is when you don't have
to have fun to enjoy yourself.

—Franklin P. Jones

You stay young as long as you can learn,
acquire new habits and suffer contradictions.

—Marie von Ebner-Eschenbach

The key to change...is to let go of fear.

—Rosanne Cash

The person who has lived the most is not
the one with the most years but the one
with the richest experiences.

—Jean Jacques Rousseau

Look up and not down; look forward and
not back; look out and not in;
and lend a hand.

—Edward Everett Hale

*Do not deprive me of my age.
I have earned it.*

—

May Sarton

Attitude

A grandmother's attitude is contagious. If she is optimistic and upbeat, the family will tend to be likewise. But, if grandmother falls prey to pessimism and doubt, the family suffers right along with her.

Wise grandmoms understand the power of positive thinking. These special women share a message of encouragement and hope with those around them, especially with their children and grandchildren. And savvy grandmothers, as they spread their happiness and optimism, can't help getting a little on themselves.

You can't turn back the clock.
But you can wind it up again.
—

Bonnie Prudden

Chapter 11
Grandmother's
Advice

The one important thing
I've learned over the years is
the difference between taking
one's work seriously and
taking one's self seriously.
The first is imperative,
and the second is disastrous.

—

Margaret Fontey

*W*ho knows more than Grandmother? Nobody! And if you don't believe it, just ask her. So we conclude with a potpourri of wisdom that would make any grandmother proud.

We carry the seeds of happiness with us
wherever we go.

—Martha Washington

Always keep that happy attitude.
Pretend that you are holding
a beautiful fragrant bouquet.

—Candice M. Pope

Live each day as it comes, and don't borrow
trouble by worrying about tomorrow.

—Dorothy Dix

Happiness walks on busy feet.

—Kitte Turmell

Without faith nothing is possible.
  With it, nothing is impossible.
       —Mary McLeod Bethune

In spite of everything I still believe that
  people are really good at heart.
  I simply can't build up my hopes on
    a foundation consisting
  of confusion, misery and death.
        —Anne Frank

The way I see it, if you want the rainbow,
  you've got to put up with the rain.
        —Dolly Parton

One thing that doesn't abide by
   majority rule is a person's conscience.
                                    —Harper Lee

If you listen to your conscience, it will serve
   you as no other friend you'll ever know.
                                    —Loretta Young

Service is the rent you pay for room
            on this earth.
                                    —Shirley Chisholm

I don't want to get to the end of my life
   and find that I just lived the length of it.
I want to have lived the width of it as well.
                                    —Diane Ackerman

Service to a just cause rewards the worker
with more real happiness and satisfaction
than any other venture of life.

—Carrie Chapman Catt

When you cease to contribute,
you begin to die.

—Eleanor Roosevelt

Believe that your tender, loving thoughts
and wishes for good have power to help the
struggling souls of earth rise higher.

—Ella Wheeler Wilcox

This is happiness; to be dissolved
into something complete and great.

—Willa Cather

The best and most beautiful things in
the world cannot be seen or even touched.
They must be felt with the human heart.

—Helen Keller

It is only possible to live happily-ever-after
on a day-to-day basis.

—Margaret Bonano

Happiness is a matter of one's most
ordinary everyday mode of consciousness,
being busy and lively and unconcerned
with self.

—Iris Murdoch

Keep what is worth keeping and with the
breath of kindness blow the rest away.

—Dinah Maria Murlock Craik

There is no good reason why we should not develop and change until the last day we live.

—Karen Horney

I tell everybody to travel and
    not get married too soon.

—Moms Mabley

The search for instant gratification
    is harmful.

—Shirley Ann Grau

The best time to make friends is before
    you need them.

—Ethel Barrymore

If I'd realized how much fun grandchildren
were, I'd have had them first!
—Faith Myers

If you don't want your children to hear what
you're saying, pretend you're talking to them.
—E. C. McKenzie

I have found the best way to give advice
to your children is to find out what they
want and then advise them to do it.
—Harry S. Truman

The best things you can give your children,
next to good habits, are good memories.

—Sydney J. Harris

Good manners will often take people where
neither money nor education will take them.

—Fanny Jackson Coppin

The end is nothing. The road is all.

—Willa Cather

Make beauty a familiar guest.

—Mary Howitt

A woman is like a tea bag. You never know
how strong she is until she gets
into hot water.
—Eleanor Roosevelt

If you think you can, you can.
If you think you can't, you're right.
—Mary Kay Ash

My grandmother used to say a day is
wasted if you don't fall over at least
once with laughter.
—Luci Swindoll

Treat the world well. It was not given to
you by your parents but lent to you
by your children.
—Ida B. Wells

Each day, look for a kernel of excitement.

—Barbara Johnson

I never really look for things.
I accept whatever God throws my way.
Whichever way God turns my feet, I go.

—Pearl Bailey

Earth's crammed with heaven.

—Elizabeth Barrett Browning

Faith can put a candle in the darkest night.

—Margaret Sangster

Dignity is like a perfume; those who use it
are scarcely conscious of it.
—Queen Christina of Sweden

Charm is simply this: the golden rule,
good manners, good grooming,
good humor, good sense,
good habits, and a good outlook.
—Loretta Young

Take the back roads instead of
the highways.
—Minnie Pearl

When young people ask me how I made it,
I say, "It's absolutely hard work.
Nobody's gonna wave a magic wand."
—Loretta Lynn